The History of
the Camera

Summit Free Public Library

Elizabeth Raum

Heinemann
LIBRARY

Chicago, Illinois

© **2008 Heinemann Library**
a division of Reed Elsevier Inc.
Chicago, Illinois

Customer Service 888-454-2279

Visit our website at www.heinemannlibrary.com

Designed by Victoria Bevan and Tower Designs Ltd.
Printed in China by South China Printing.

11 10 09 08 07
10 9 8 7 6 5 4 3 2 1

Library of Congress Cataloging-in-Publication Data

Raum, Elizabeth.
   The history of the camera / Elizabeth Raum.
      p. cm. -- (Inventions that changed the world)
   Includes bibliographical references and index.
   ISBN 978-1-4034-9647-8 (hc) -- ISBN 978-1-4034-9653-9 (pb)
   1. Cameras--History--Juvenile literature. I. Title.
   TR250.R38 2007
   771.309--dc22

J
NF

                         2006039527

Acknowledgments
The author and publishers are grateful to the following for permission to reproduce copyright material: p. **4** Getty Images/Robert Harding World Imagery, p. **5** Corbis/The State Russian Museum, p. **6** Science & Society Picture Library/ Science Museum, p. **7** Science & Society Picture Library/NMPFT, p. **8** Corbis/Michael Freeman, p. **9** The Art Archive/Culver Pictures, p. **10** Topham Picturepoint, p. **11** Science & Society Picture Library/National Museum of Photography, p. **12** akg-images, p. **13** Corbis/Bettman, p. **14** Topham Picturepoint, p. **15** Science Photo Library/Library of Congress, p. **16** Topham Picturepoint, p. **17** Advertising Archives, p. **18** Science & Society Picture Library/National Museum of Photography, p. **19** Corbis/H. Armstrong Roberts, p. **20** Science & Society Picture Library/National Museum of Photography, p. **21** Advertising Archives, p. **22** Science Photo Library/Planetary Visions Ltd, p. **23** Getty Images/ Photographer's Choice (Alamy), p. **24** akg-images, p. **25** Science Photo Library/Cordelia Molloy), p. **26** Masterfile/ Michael Goldman (Getty/Photodisc), p. **27** Photolibrary.com/Pacific Stock/Carl Roessler (Alamy/Paul Springett).

Cover photograph reproduced with permission of Corbis/Hulton Deutsch Collection.

Every effort has been made to contact copyright holders of any material reproduced in this book. Any omissions will be rectified in subsequent printings if notice is given to the publisher.

Disclaimer
All Internet addresses (URLs) given in this book were valid at the time of going to press. However, due to the dynamic nature of the Internet, some addresses may have changed or ceased to exist since publication. While the author and the publishers regret any inconvenience this may cause readers, no responsibility for any such changes can be accepted by either the author or the publishers.

Contents

Some words are shown in bold, **like this**. You can find out what they mean by looking in the glossary.

Before Cameras

People everywhere enjoy looking at pictures. From the earliest days, people have drawn pictures. Pictures help us remember places, people, and events.

People drew this picture in a cave in France thousands of years ago.

Painting a picture like this one sometimes took weeks or months.

Before there were cameras, artists painted pictures. Many of the paintings were beautiful, but they took a long time to finish. Sometimes the paintings did not look real.

The First Camera

For many years, people wanted to make a camera. The **camera obscura** came first. It made a picture, but the picture had to be copied by hand onto paper.

This machine, called a camera obscura, was a very early kind of camera.

This is Joseph Niépce's first photo. It was fuzzy, but it was a start.

Joseph Niépce, of France, had a new idea. He used **chemicals** to make a picture on a piece of **metal**. In 1826 he took a **photograph** (also called photo) of the buildings and fields outside his window. He had **invented** the camera.

Daguerre Makes Better Photos

Louis Daguerre, who was also from France, worked with Niépce. In 1839 Daguerre found a way to make the photos taken on Niépce's camera last a long time. He called his photos **daguerreotypes**.

Louis Daguerre's first camera looked like a wooden box.

Most early daguerreotype photos like this one were of people.

Newspaper writers wrote stories about Daguerre's new way to make photos. People wanted to learn more. Daguerre wrote a book explaining how to make daguerreotypes. The book was printed in eight languages.

Talbot's Photos on Paper

Louis Daguerre's photos were printed on **metal**. In 1839 William Henry Fox Talbot, an **inventor** from England, found a way to print photos on paper. We still print photos on paper today.

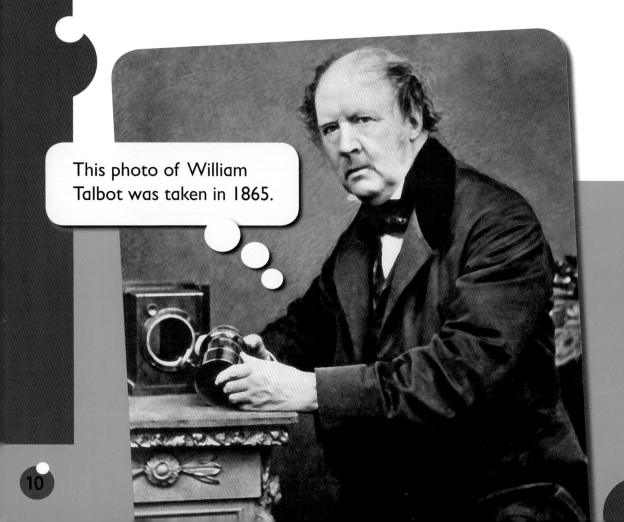

This photo of William Talbot was taken in 1865.

Talbot's first photo was called *The Handshake*.

Talbot learned how to make more than one copy of a **photograph**. He printed a book of nature pictures in 1844. It was the first book with photographs.

Using Cameras

In the middle of the 1800s, **photography studios** opened all over Europe and the United States. Children and entire families **posed** for photos. People sent the photos to friends. They kept the photos to look at in later years.

These children posed for a photo in a photography studio.

A photographer took this school photo in 1885.

Photographers began taking cameras out into the world. They traveled to places most people could not go. These pictures helped people learn what was happening around the world.

George Eastman's Idea

Many of the first cameras were very big and hard to carry. These cameras used heavy **plates** instead of **film**. **Inventors** around the world tried to make cameras that were smaller and easier to use.

This huge camera was used to take a photo of a train.

People taking photos needed a big camera, a stand to hold the camera, and heavy plates. George Eastman, of the United States, wanted to find an easier way to take photos. In 1884 he **invented** film on a roll.

George Eastman made it easier for people to take photos.

Cameras for Everyone

George Eastman began a company called Kodak. In 1888 the first Kodak camera was sold. It was smaller than earlier cameras. Many people bought the first Kodak camera even though it cost a lot of money.

The first Kodak camera came with its own case.

THE BROWNIE.

Not a Toy. Takes splendid Photographs, $2\frac{1}{4}$ by $2\frac{1}{4}$ inches. Complete with Handbook of Instructions. Price only **5/-**

Of all Photographic Dealers, or from—
KODAK, Limited,

43, Clerkenwell Road, E.C.;
60, Cheapside, E.C.;
115, Oxford Street, W.;
and 171-3, Regent Street, W.

Brownie cameras were sold around the world.

In 1900 Kodak **invented** a camera called the Brownie. Kodak's Brownie camera was easy to use. Millions of children and adults bought Brownie cameras. Kodak sold Brownies for 70 years.

Flash and Color

Cameras got better over time. Oskar Barnack, from Germany, **invented** a new kind of camera. He called it a Leica. It was the first **35 millimeter camera**. In 1924 people started buying Leica cameras.

By the 1930s, cameras came in many shapes and sizes.

This news photographer is using a camera with a big flash.

In 1930 the flash camera was invented. The flash of light let **photographers** take photos in dark places. By 1936 a new kind of **film** made color photos possible. More people bought color film than black and white.

Instant Pictures

In 1944 Edwin Land, of the United States, took a photo of his three-year-old daughter. She asked to see the photo right away. That gave him an idea.

The first Polaroid cameras folded up when not in use.

WOW!

When Pop opens up his Christmas present and sees it's a Polaroid Land Camera he'll bust out from ear to ear.

But when he snaps that first picture... and 60 seconds later takes the finished print out of the back of the camera—there'll be no holding him. By turkey time he'll have the greatest collection of Christmas Day pictures you ever saw. Here's why:

First of all, there's a great new *panchromatic* Polaroid Land Film that gives you the richest blacks and snowiest whites you've ever seen. Details that are razor sharp. Delicate flesh tones that make' your pictures of people look amazingly lifelike.

Secondly, with *this* camera you eliminate the guesswork. If Suzy blinks or Eddie makes a face, you shoot another picture on the spot.

None of that disappointment at the drugstore a week later when you find out the shots you wanted most were fuzzy, too dark, or just plain blanks.

Another thing. With this new film, Polaroid Land pictures don't fade—they last just like any other pictures. And you can get all the copies and enlargements you want.

Look. Every year you've been going to get him something extra special. This is the Christmas to do it. (Polaroid Land Cameras are priced from $69.95 or only $1.19 a week.) POLAROID CORP., CAMBRIDGE, MASS.

POLAROID® LAND CAMERA WITH NEW PANCHROMATIC FILM

In 1947 Land **invented** an **instant** camera. It was called a Polaroid. Minutes after the picture was snapped, a photo came out of the camera.

Digital Cameras

In the 1970s, **astronauts** wanted to take photos in space and send them back to Earth quickly. **Inventors** made the digital camera. Digital cameras do not need **film**. The photos are stored on a tiny computer disk inside the camera.

Digital cameras show people how Earth looks from space.

Today many cell phones can take photos.

It took time to make the digital camera smaller and easy to use. In 1991 Kodak began selling digital cameras to the public. In 2000 a company in Japan put a camera in a cell phone. Now many companies make camera phones.

Cameras that Help People

Today we can use cameras to help keep us safe. Cameras help guard banks from robbers. Cameras in schools help guard students from strangers. Cameras watch busy roads so that the police know when there are problems.

This camera takes photos of everyone who passes by it.

Doctors also use cameras. Doctors use X-ray cameras to see broken bones. In 2005 an **inventor** put a camera in a pill. It lets doctors see inside a person's body.

A pill camera is very tiny.

How Cameras Changed Life

Before cameras, people had to draw or paint pictures. Now cameras make it easy to have photos every day. Cameras also make it easy to remember the past. We can look at old photos to learn about life long ago.

Today it is easy to take photos.

This **photographer** is taking pictures underwater with a special camera.

Cameras take us to places we cannot go. They take us into space or underwater. In the future, cameras will take even better photos. They will be even easier to use.

Timeline

1826 Joseph Niépce **invents** the camera.

1839 Louis Daguerre invents **daguerreotypes**.

1839 William Talbot prints photos on paper.

1884 George Eastman invents **film** on a roll.

1888 Kodak camera is for sale.

1924 Oskar Barnack's **35 millimeter camera** is for sale.

1930 Flash camera is invented.

1935 Color film is invented.

1947 Edwin Land invents the Polaroid **instant** camera.

1975 Digital camera is invented.

1991 Digital camera is for sale.

2000 Camera phone is invented.

2005 Pill camera is first used.

World Map Activity

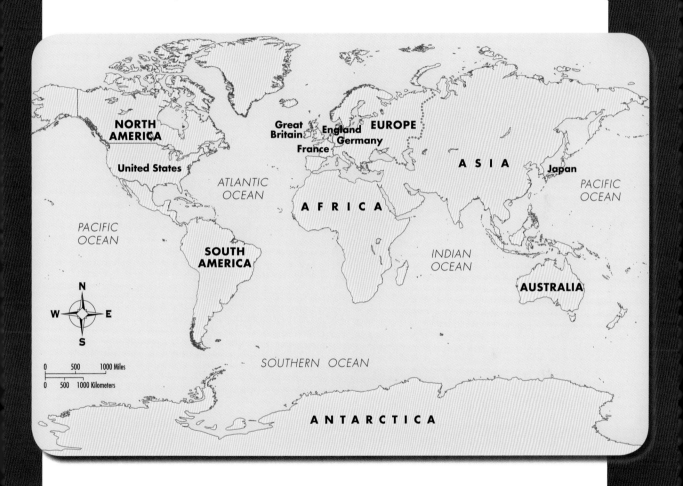

The countries talked about in this book are labeled on this world map. Try to find each **inventor's** country on the map.

Find Out More

Books

Friedman, Debra. *Picture This: Fun Photography and Crafts*. Tonawanda, NY: Kids Can Press, 2003.

Gillis, Jennifer Blizin. *George Eastman*. Chicago: Heinemann Library, 2004.

An older reader can help you with this book:
Hills, Larry. *The Camera*. Mankato, MN: Capstone, 2005.

Websites

Kids News Room - George Eastman
http://www.kidsnewsroom.org/elmer/infoCentral/frameset/
inventors/eastman/index.html

Utah State Historical Society - Photo Facts & Fun
http://historyforkids.utah.gov/fun_and_games/photos/
index.html

Glossary

35 millimeter camera (35 mm camera) camera that uses special film that is 35 millimeters wide to take good pictures

astronaut someone who travels in space

camera obscura type of early camera that could not store photos

chemical substance mixed with other substances to make something happen, such as make a photo

daguerreotype photo on metal

film roll of thin plastic used in a camera to store photos

instant happen right away

invent make something that did not exist before

inventor someone who makes something that did not exist before

metal hard, shiny material that melts when it is heated

photograph (photo) picture taken by a camera

photographer someone who uses a camera to take photos

photography studio room or building where pictures are taken

plate heavy piece of metal needed by early cameras to make a photo

pose stay still for a picture

Index